MANN

THE
GREAT
Co.

To Iaki, Nicole, Maryellen, and everyone at Candlewick.
Thanks for working your magic once again.
M. R.

Dedicated to my magical wife,
and in honor of Adelaide, may you all realize your
dreams with hard work and a touch of magic.
I. B.

First edition 2016

Library of Congress Catalog Card Number 2015934260
ISBN 978-0-7636-6841-9

16 17 18 19 20 21 LEO 10 9 8 7 6 5 4 3 2 1

Printed in Heshan, Guangdong, China

This book was typeset in Century Old Style, Cheltenham Condensed,
and Copperplate Gothic, and drawn by the illustrator.
The illustrations were done in pencil and colored digitally.

Candlewick Press
99 Dover Street
Somerville, Massachusetts 02144

visit us at www.candlewick.com

ANYTHING BUT ORDINARY

ADDIE

The TRUE·STORY·OF ADELAIDE HERRMANN

QUEEN of MAGIC

MARA ROCKLIFF

illustrated by IACOPO BRUNO

CANDLEWICK PRESS

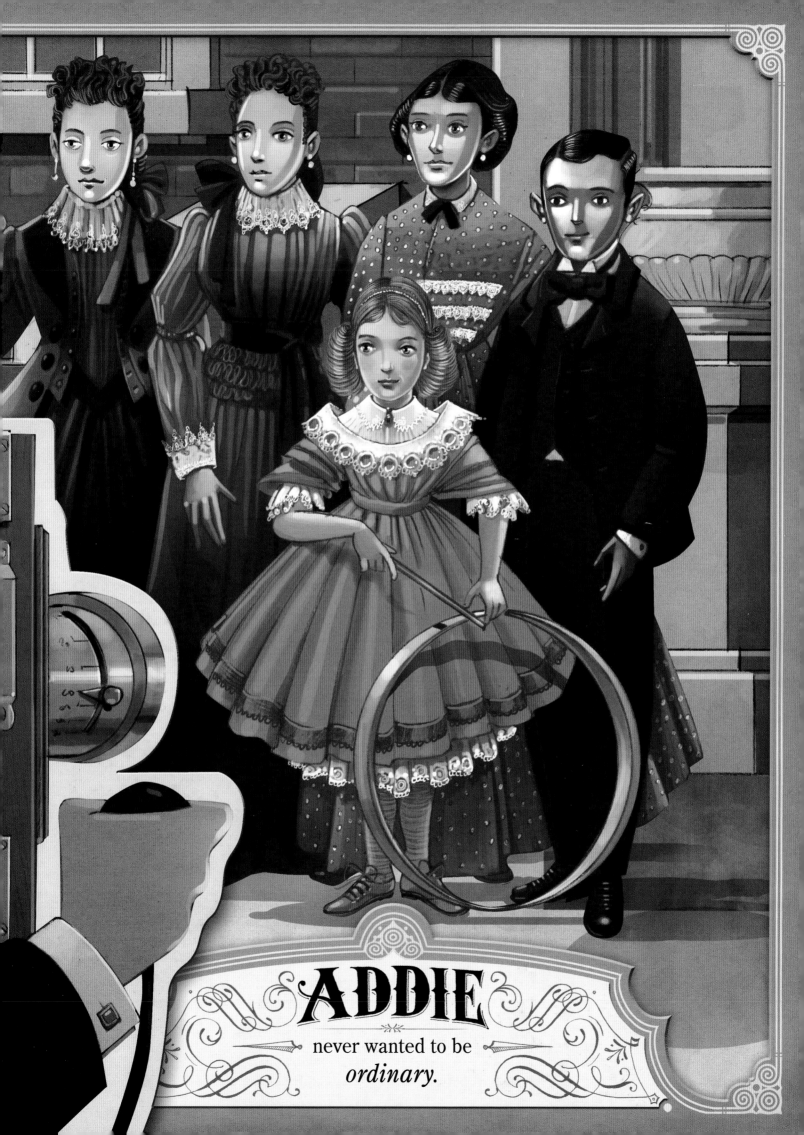

ADDIE

never wanted to be *ordinary*.

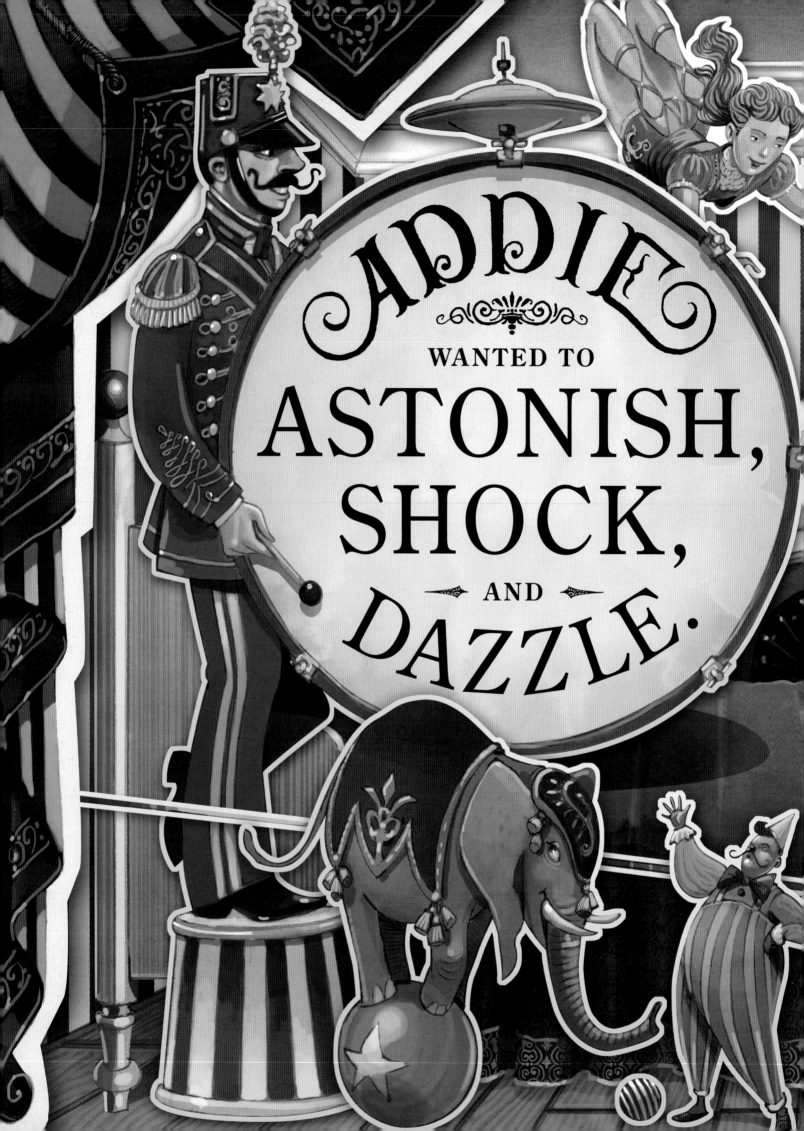

ADDIE

WANTED TO

ASTONISH,
SHOCK,
AND
DAZZLE.

One day, she saw an advertisement in the newspaper.

THE ILLUSTRATE

WANTED—YOUNG

TO LEARN D

Secretly, she sewed herself a
dancing dress and joined the troupe.

When Addie told her family
what she was doing, they were
SHOCKED.

Our Addie?
On the stage?
In front of everyone?
IN TIGHTS?

But then they saw her dance—
and Addie was
ASTONISHINGLY good.

Addie liked being a prima ballerina.
Still, floating gracefully across the
stage felt just the tiniest bit . . .

ordinary.

Lots of girls could dance,
Addie told herself.
But how many dared hop on the
newfangled invention called—

The
BONESHAKER!!!

Soon Addie could be seen
pedaling merrily around . . .
in the most SHOCKING
costume . . .
doing *extraordinary* tricks.

Addie DAZZLED crowds in
London . . .
Brussels . . .
Paris . . .

Next thing Addie knew, she found
herself crossing the ocean to

AMERICA.

On board the ship, she met an elegant
young man. His name was Alexander.
But the world knew him as

HERRMANN
THE GREAT.

ADDIE was DAZZLED.
She told Alexander she would like to marry him.

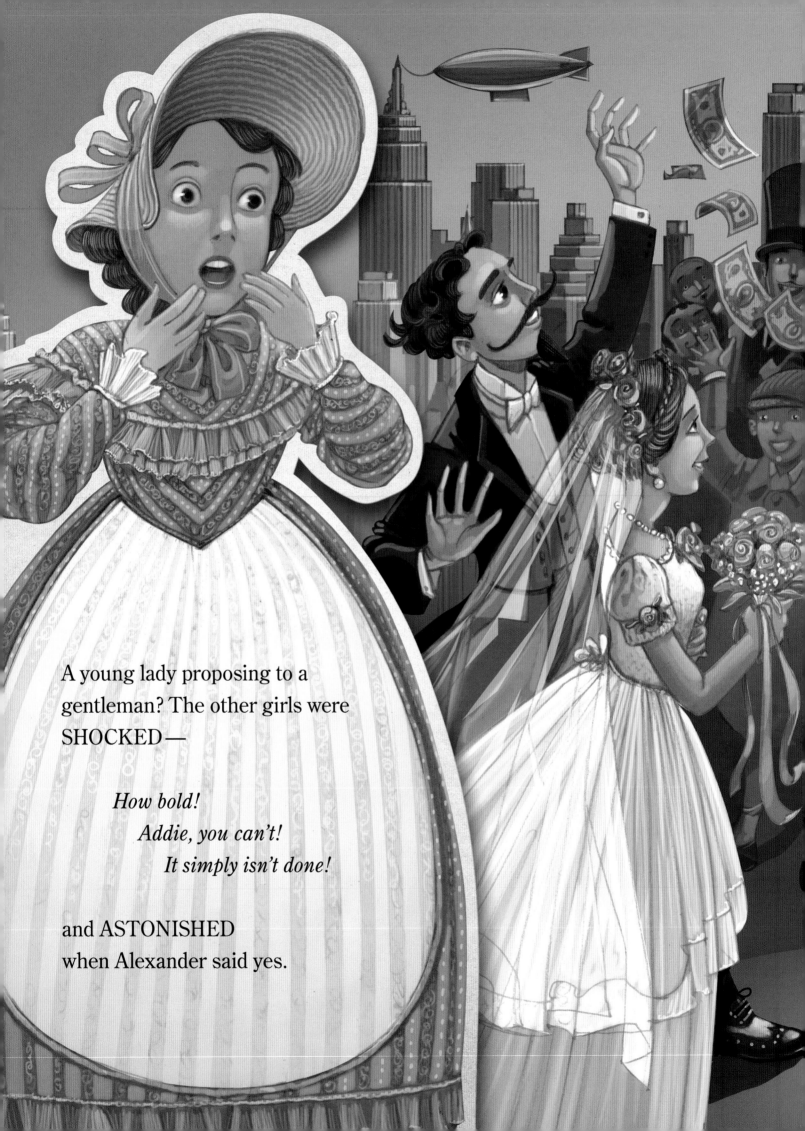

A young lady proposing to a
gentleman? The other girls were
SHOCKED—

How bold!
Addie, you can't!
It simply isn't done!

and ASTONISHED
when Alexander said yes.

The mayor of New York himself
performed the wedding ceremony.
But how to pay his fee?

Fortunately, money had a way
of turning up!

Alexander was no *ordinary* husband.

He set fire to Addie.
He chopped off her head.
He made her vanish
(poof!)
into thin air.

The two of them got
along splendidly.

Together, they
ASTONISHED,
SHOCKED,
and
DAZZLED
audiences around
the globe.

They hired more performers for their show:

A JUGGLER —

A FAMILY OF

TUMBLERS —

A VENTRILOQUIST —

and
THE BEAUTIFUL
GERALDINE,
who climbed into a
cannon's mouth and
BOOM!

One night, Geraldine vanished. *(Poof!)*
It wasn't part of the act—she had run off before the audience arrived!
"Shoot *me* from the cannon," Addie offered.
Alexander was SHOCKED. Addie wasn't an acrobat!
She'd never tried this trick.
Still, they both knew that the show must go on, so . . .

BOOM!

Even Addie was a bit
ASTONISHED
when she
landed safely in the net.

Almost nothing frightened Addie.
One thing, only one, could make her
tremble in her spangled slippers—

THE
BULLET-CATCHING
TRICK.

Very few magicians had ever mastered
this thrilling, death-defying act.
It DAZZLED audiences—

and TERRIFIED Addie.

She knew it was truly dangerous. Magicians had been killed when it went wrong. Addie begged Alexander not to do that trick.

At last he agreed, and Addie felt happy knowing her husband was safe.

But fate had a
SHOCK up its sleeve.
One night, on the
train to a performance,
Alexander's heart
quietly gave out.
This time, there would
be no ASTONISHING
escape from death.

For ADDIE, the magic had vanished.

Yet she knew that without **HERRMANN THE GREAT,** all the other performers would be out of work.

Theater managers would
lock their doors
and disappointed children
would be turned away.
No! The show must go on.
BUT HOW?

1897.

"I WILL DO IT MYSELF!"

Addie announced.

Everyone was SHOCKED.

A woman magician?
Who ever heard of such a thing?
No one will come!

Addie had never cared what others thought.

But now she worried they were right.

What if nobody came?

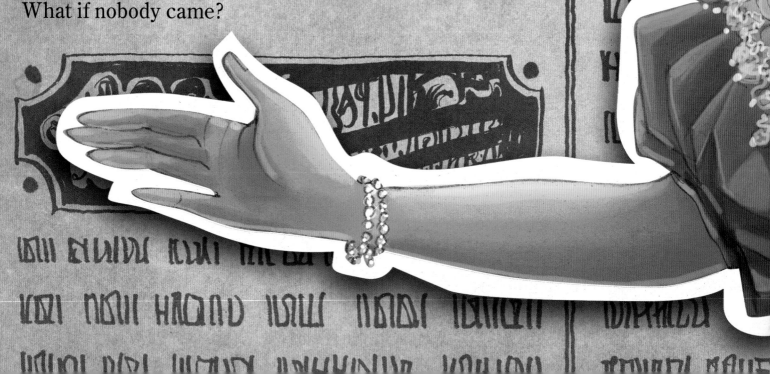

Addie knew she could do anything
HERRMANN THE GREAT had done.
She could pull rabbits from the air.
She could make a bright shower of
    oranges and candies rain onto the stage.
She could turn a painting of a beautiful
    young girl into a real girl, and back again.
But if an audience did not appear . . .
            (poof!)
    it wouldn't matter what Addie could do.

She needed an act so SHOCKING,
    so ASTONISHING—
    so DAZZLING, THRILLING,
    and DEATH-DEFYING—
    NO ONE could stay home.

It had to be . . .

THE BULLET-CATCHING TRICK.

The night came.
The theater was packed.
Addie stood alone,
facing a squad of soldiers,
loaded rifles raised.

Ready!

Addie held up a fragile
china plate. Several
frightened men rushed
for the exit.

Aim!
A woman screamed
and fainted.
Addie trembled
but stood firm.

FIRE!

Thanks to Addie,
the show DID go on—
for thirty more years!

Addie created many
DAZZLING, ASTONISHING
tricks of her own.
No one could ever guess what new
illusion she had up her sleeve.

But Addie being Addie,
everybody knew for sure . . .

it would be

ANYTHING·BUT·ORDINARY.

ADDIE
THE GREAT

ONCE UPON A TIME, the world's most famous magicians were named Herrmann. There was Carl Herrmann, his much younger brother Alexander, their nephew Leon—and, of course, the Queen of Magic: Alexander's widow, Adelaide.

Adelaide was born Adele Scarsez in London on August 11, 1853. Addie's parents were Belgian, and she and her older siblings grew up speaking French—a skill that came in handy when Addie met a handsome Parisian magician on a ship.

Addie and Alexander had a lot in common. They were both bold and adventurous. They both adored animals. (Pets they collected on their travels—and used in their show—included ostriches, monkeys, chameleons, macaws, pigs, chickens, rabbits, goats, puppies, and a snake that got loose on a train and wrapped itself around the ankle of a traveling salesman, frightening him nearly to death.) And they both had a way of making audiences fall in love with them the instant they appeared onstage.

In her sixty-five years of magic, Adelaide met everyone in show business. The silent-film star Buster Keaton played vaudeville with her when he was six years old. Adelaide counted as friends the actress Sarah Bernhardt, songwriter Oscar Hammerstein, and showmen P. T. Barnum and Buffalo Bill Cody.

Among magicians, Adelaide reigned unchallenged as the Queen of Magic. Sensational escape artist Harry Houdini was a fan. Alexander's archrival, Harry Kellar, saw Addie's show and praised her act as "perfect in every detail." Adelaide encouraged other girls and women to learn magic and even revealed the secrets to a few tricks in *Woman's Home Companion* magazine. When Addie died, in 1932, her funeral was crowded with magicians. Over her coffin, they solemnly broke her magic wand. The Queen was gone.

SEARCHING FOR ADDIE

AFTER ADDIE DIED, the world forgot the Queen of Magic. She had written about her adventures with Alexander and on her own in a memoir called *Sixty-Five Years of Magic*, but nobody wanted to publish it. The carefully typed pages in a leather-covered notebook passed to Addie's favorite niece, Adele, who tucked them away with family photographs and other treasures.

The years went by. Books about the history of magic barely mentioned Addie, except as Alexander's wife and assistant. Generations of girls grew up thinking all the great magicians had been men.

One of those girls was Margaret Steele, who became a stage magician anyway. Even though she'd never heard of Addie, Margaret came up with some of the same tricks, such as making billiard balls appear and disappear at her fingertips.

One night, after Margaret's performance, a man rushed into her dressing room. His name was James Hamilton, and he was a fellow magician and a historian of magic. James told Margaret that watching her show was like seeing Adelaide Herrmann come back to life. Margaret said, "Who?"

With help from James, Margaret began piecing together the story of Addie's life. She eventually learned enough to re-create part of Addie's act, with stirring music, graceful gestures, and flowing robes. But she still wanted to know more.

For ten years, Margaret hunted for Addie's memoir. Nobody knew where it was. People told her that it probably didn't exist.

At last, the leather notebook surfaced among the belongings of Adele's descendants. Margaret published the memoir, together with various items from her own collection, under the title *Adelaide Herrmann: Queen of Magic* (Bramble Books, 2012). This book was the main source for *Anything But Ordinary Addie*, along with two earlier articles* and several extremely helpful and informative e-mails from Margaret Steele.

Thanks to Margaret, the Queen of Magic lives again.

---

* "Adelaide Herrmann" by James Hamilton (*Genii: The Conjurors' Magazine*, August 2000, pp. 41–52) and "Adelaide Herrmann and the Society of American Magicians" by Margaret Steele (*M-U-M Magazine*, May 2011, pp. 44–47).

SECRETS OF THE BULLET-CATCHING TRICK REVEALED!

How did Addie do it?
Find out at www.mararockliff.com/bullet.html.